Some Help from the Dead

Some Help from the Dead

poems by

Ally Acker

Red Hen Press | Pasadena, CA

Some Help from the Dead

Book design by Mark E. Cull
Book layout by Kathrine Davidson

ISBN: 978-1-59709-519-8

Artwork by Remedios Varo: The Encounter (1950), Towards the Tower (1960), Hairy Locomotion (1959), Weaving the Mantle of the World (1961), Creation of the Birds (1957). Copyright © 2010 by the Estate of Remedios Varo. Permissions granted by Alexandra Gruen.

Photographs of Russia courtesy of Victoria Ward © 2010. Estate of Nicholas Avinoff.

The Annenberg Foundation, the California Arts Council, the James Irvine Foundation, the Los Angeles County Arts Commission, the National Endowment for the Arts, Sony Pictures, and Department of Cultural Affairs partially support Red Hen Press.

First Edition

Published by Red Hen Press
Pasadena, CA
www.redhen.org

Acknowledgements

Grateful acknowledgment is made by the author to the following periodicals in which a number of these poems first appeared:

Ailanthus, Audemus, The American Voice, The Antioch Review, The Current, Folio, Ms Magazine, Oxford Magazine, The Piedmont Literary Review, Plexus, Ploughshares, Poetry Kanto (Japan), *Sojourner, The South Dakota Review, The Southwest Review, The Sun, Woman of Power, WordWrights.*

Line: "What falls away is always. And is near."
Theodore Roethke, "The Waking" from Collected Poems of Theodore Roethke. Copyright 1953 by Theodore Roethke. Reprinted with the permission of Doubleday, a division of Random House, Inc.

Heartfelt thanks to Anna Yatsko's red-haired boy for his careful reading of these poems.

And most especially to Mark and Kate . . . your miraculous hard work, your years of friendship, your lovely, lovely press. Thank you.

For Sally Redmond

(1947 - 1988)

Paul Hinckley

(1955 - 1988)

Pat Van Rhyn

(1925 - 2009)

Dad

(1920 - 1990)

and all my dead dears

Contents

A Clouding of Angels

De lusion

Insomnia

Weaving the Mantle of the World

Five poems inspired by the art of Remedios Varo

Respite

To live with ghosts requires solitude.

—Anne Michaels

A Clouding of Angels

Listen to the dead. They are trying to help you.

—Alicia Ostriker, "Sheba's Proverbs"

In the House of My Dead Father

When I was left again for someone
better someone younger someone
whose ghosts did not violate the regal
impenetrable
pecking order   I came home
to the house of my dead father

Donned his argyle socks
the extra large white fruit-of-the-loom T
the yellow V-Neck sweater, moth-
eaten under one sleeve for Sundays

I came
believing here was something I left
something familiar
in some cupboard somewhere
that look we shared when my mother blathered
another inanity

I stayed
because now the house had to be
painted and the chipped
patio rebricked and the wailing attic
purged of the besieging
thunderous weight

Somewhere down in the basement
I had lost a piece
I ravaged
mining and infiltrating the dark like a mole buried
by her last chances

I had abdicated the sanctimonious palate
of the self
all I had become
because somewhere deep
in this house its walls its vast
carnivorous moanings

was the answer to everything
I thought I left
thought he knew thought
he'd let me in on now that he
had gotten to a place

where the secret once folded and stuffed
and buried beneath tufted cotton
could be unveiled to all its original
wonder   And that I

could finally become
that being   that one
he was always seeing when he looked
right at me   straight
into my eyes

Maybe, Sal

I've just arrived. Put down my bags. Sally passes
in the hall on her way to somewhere
Leap on tiptoes, *INHALE HER TO ME*, *I miss you!* I say
You don't, she says. That indomitable British. *You miss talking*
to me.

I feel her

There would be cheating and betrayals, suicide and death
But that would be later
Through death, through sleep, through nearly thirty years
I swear, I feel her

You were dreaming, you say.

So maybe I was
Maybe everything we know and love and lose at the long empty death
of it
is just goddam gone and tallies to nothing
Maybe we evaporate, and with us our sad, pathetic, eviscerated tales
Maybe all the import of our dramas piss away dull like air
escaping from a slow pin hole

ENTROPY
The Crying of Lot 49

Or maybe Sal climbed up through death,
through her lonely eviscerated crypt, repudiating hell and all that is finished
and came to see me
Maybe when she plundered and fucked me 69
on Jolie's couch in DC in 1980, till I screamed in the rapturous violence

Maybe, just maybe, she crawled inside of me
made her nest of thistle and rock
Maybe she found a home that very day
and quite simply
decided to stay

in those days

in those days there was a kind of sageness to us
drifting   going sideways   going straight
it didn't matter
we were looking for love

purpose only meant a thing with a handrail
we held onto it
it took us somewhere
and it kept us from falling

For Sally Reymond

(1947 - 1988)

Faery,
mystical pungent
flask of brandy
and driftlessness

You haunt me in hotel rooms
Bawdy

salamander of so many slivered
nights, stealing my puella
when you drown your own.

Who cast you, drunken
ashes and all, into the sea
of a country that never claimed you?

Home was the dark tomb
of L.A. . . . or my boss' darkly paneled
office on Madison, where you spread me

your thirstiest fan
of toxic confessions. Brandy
made you say, *I'll carve your grave,*
'Acker dreamed.'

But now, Sparrow, it is you,
premature in your messy mausoleum
doing the dreaming.

The soft peace
my hands gave you. *Faery*
you'd say, then lift my chalice
to your flaming

orifice. *Faery*
then the spontaneous combustion
drove you inside me.
Sal

says the unmarked stone
that will never again keep still,
Reymond,
I would have come
and come and come for you.
Why was one sweet elixir
never enough?

Firebird

(for sally, again)

". . . the beating of the heart
makes one impatient . . ."
—Jayanta Mayapatra

You were the firebird no one could catch
But ran after you I did, longing, as we all long for
darkness and ineffable beauty. As one longs
for the river always on its way to somewhere else.
To refuse to lie down one's arms in defeat
and call it peace.

I am a child again. Time has ceased.
The loon stirs us with its long note,
even in our deepest sleep. (Is it possible
in loneliness to find home? Is the long
tunnel to death only the shadow of a clock?
It arms pushing, useless as a calendar,
far far back to childhood, sputtering the loose change
of our memories, back back all the way back
to Milky Way and stars)

Yoshico

I had a friend who had a friend named Yoshico.
Yoshico had a Tatami house.
One day, we snuggled
into Yoshico's futon and willed ourselves invisible.
The workmen came in, but we didn't care.
There were the large, lovely words that filled our mouths,
Hydrangea Rhododendron Delphinium

There were the fragrances of the body

To please her, I went on the stage.
Is you my woman, Bess?

Lilac Honeysuckle
In time, the air changed.
George and Vicki put on their cruel faces
A Robin sat on a branch and covered the moon.
The seasons, and again your door was lost to me.
But once there was the girl who reigned
marvelous and complete,
in the face of the exotic,
the ineffable.

The Hours

for Rene Wyndham

We green and dream of youth . . .
—Joan Campbell

There are not enough hours

A friend I know in Dorset
so eclectic she beads jewels,
philosophizes De Beauvoir, and manages still to believe
in heaven
I've done a study, she says,

What with our hair, the elderly, frantic workings
of the collective unconscious
we need 280 hours whereas
we've only got 168

There are not enough hours

for the deep threads of Hollyhocks
to tell us how simple
happiness has always been

or the great greening of lambs
in this poem already lost
to the field

You are on the train, you see,
and the field, the lambs
must be left
behind

The friend too now, is miles away
(does she still exist? was she real?) but we must
move on

You're older now.
It takes longer to make you cry
as you watch the lamb, the field, the friend
dissolve into what
may not have existed at all

But there it is:
the miracles the hours brought,
cramming and filling and rearranging us
(a scone here, a peppermint tea there)
in spite of their lack,

there has been a birth, a journey,
a mysterious transformation,
a once and never quite like this again
tiny sheep

I Do

We are alone. All 89.8 million of us. Some of us are alone with entitlement. Some of us walk the earth and think we're trespassing.

I am married like no other. I am married to wind, birds, breath. Last night, the woman I marry spoons me until I cannot breathe. I float away dreaming of wings. The minute I am gone, I implore my brother, who wears the face of my old roommate, Margaret, to fix me up with any woman he can find. *It is impossible*, he says, he's going to Europe. But he is a lesbian, why doesn't he understand?

Sometimes I am a gay man trapped in a lesbian's body. I love mauve the way others love security or ice cream. I can design a living room Martha Stewart would assassinate for.

Sometimes, the little biker dyke comes out. She's cutting my lawn, fixes my plumbing, and commands me to spread for her so she can fuck me faceless. But first, she makes me beg for it. That's the best part.

Other nights, I dream of a man who makes love more tenderly than any bull dyke dreamed possible. The male in me is married to words that begin with 'C'. Confusion is number one. I marry confusion as others marry skin. Commitment rhymes with Cancer. This man is married to flight the way others are married to breath. By now, the cancer has spread through his life in epidemic proportions. He is the only one who does not know.

Last night, I married the deer hit on the side of the road—her 'O' mouth yawping soundless to the terrible dark. I stand stupid and dumb as death spits at me, then carries her breath. I love her like no other. I envy her. I marry her so she will not die in vain. I marry her so she will have been beloved.

I am married the way my old maid Aunt Hannah is married, with solitude
breathing down her days, her tiny apartment, its shrinking rooms.
When I say to her, *It's been so long. It will be good to see you.* She replies,
There's nothing much to see. Solitude has overtaken her. She has already moved out.
Soon, there will not even be room for the furniture.

When I turn, the woman I've married wears the face of my father.
I thought you were dead. I say. *I am*, he says. *What is it like?*
It's just like here, he says, *except there is no pain.*
I want to live where he is.

I wake in my childhood room. I wake to my dead father.
But now I am fifty, and this is no dream.

I wake to the lover who left me for the incest victim.
Me, the rapidly vanishing self   suffocating beneath a tsunami of vanished
accomplishments. *Leaving* she said, *because I never met anyone*
with a worst childhood than mine.

This is her new lover's most stellar asset.

The incest woman is my replacement magnet,
the one huffed and puffed and fucked until
my lover is blown out of a twenty year heterosexual internment

I hate penises, she says when we first meet . . . *Shriveled old men. Not beautiful . . .*
like you . . . Married for the GI bill, she says. *You know,*
(she smiles now in that loose lipped way she knows makes me hungry),
Health benefits.

Then she takes me, and I let her,
Is you my woman, Bess? she says.
To prove I am

I lie and I spread for her, stupid and silent. This is how she likes me.
All the liquids absorbed. Everything taken in like a sponge.
No messes. Nothing fecund left to the brown fields. The blue herons lift,
their wings wild with applause. The moon turns creamy. Every one gets excited.

Then, it's over.

She goes easy now. She knows
my body belongs to her no matter what she does.

Later she says, *It was all illusion, Ally.* Her face absent. Relinquished.
With a clear conscience, she can now fuck the next one
at the door.

Some are entitled. Some trespass.
Some are married, pledged beyond the bonds of the body
and stay.

Renunciation is not letting go of the things of this world,
said Suzuki Roshi, *but accepting that they go away.*

Still Life With Manageable Object

Borderline Personality.

It doesn't sound so bad. It sounds as though
you're on the verge of something.
Something daring and creative. It sounds
as though one hasn't quite made up
one's mind about which country
to land in

Sort of like Tourette's,
which sounds kind of like a dance
from the 17th century.
Not like *Fuck, Piss, Tits, Shit*
Not like that.

Borderline.

Doesn't sound like you're
empty inside, need somebody, anybody,
body as object, to merge with every
second, to fill you up, to fill
the blankness left by mad witch
Mother. Doesn't matter who's

in the bed—just so it's someone
to build you up, never
leave, someone you can predict
and control, someone just a little
worse off in their head, a little farther off
balance, so you can feel a little more okay

(Fuck Shit Piss Tits)

Let's dance

That's what you said to me at the Chelsea
in NY at 3 AM by the jukebox that was playing,
"*I had the time of my life . . .*"
Let's dance, Al

And then later, in the flea-eaten bed,
god knows who the hell had
been in, *Go ahead, Al,*
as I fucked you, desperately trying
to keep you from running again,
Go ahead. Pleasure yourself. Do it.

Six months later, you'd be
saying it to the alcoholic incest
victim ten years your junior living
down the block.
Go ahead, Pody. Come on baby,
Fuck me.

Then, when I caught you,
It just happened, Al
That's what you said. Your face
calm and blank, as though you were cutting
carrots and a stranger walked in.
It just happened.

Like Tourette's. Like an unavoidable
car crash.
Ummm, Someone said to me later,
Sounds like a
Borderline.
Typical Borderline.

Such a simple word for such
a far off land.
It's no where near Mexico.
It's no where in this stratosphere.
Now, you live there, with Pody.

Your house, a carbon copy
of the one you had with George
for twenty years.
My life so small, you said
when we met, like you were desperate
to get out.

Now, same small town

Same dance

Same empty bed with manageable object
to squeeze
to play and pretend with
in the dark.

My Father

I thought I'd miss him but he whispers still
In a dream, on the phone, I hear the sound,
Do you think you're cheating yourself of heat?
Pay the man to do what he must and be done.
The ice is slicker than it used to be.

The black cat crawls and the window stirs.
Her paws on the ice, but not a sound.
If only we could hear what the man once heard.
If only our ears could lean toward the ground.
The ice is slicker than it used to be.

At home there are calls from the angels we kept.
From seeds, some left, some stayed and were found.
(*If only the grass and the moon could sleep.*)
We miss that wind, the secrets it honed.
The ice is slicker than it used to be.

My father was once
But my father is me

A Clouding of Angels

In Bruce and Yoshico's bed
you hid me until the voices of the workmen
(so near to our love!) were rendered
invisible

In such a great enveloping
a clouding of angels!

It was only a moment, but I found a voice!
A whisper of wings
barely seen

Now, so many years gone, still
that debris.
Is it possible?

Those workmen? These angels?
*This field? These stars?**

**Line from an unpublished poem by Joan Campbell*

DE LUSION

What falls away is always. And is near.

—Theodore Roethke

The Laundromat

Every time you go down a road, it changes into something else.
You think you're on your way to do the laundry, and then a face

will smile at you. She's pretty. She asks for a walk.
Pretty soon you're in Mozambique or China.

The peasants are rising up and all you wanted
was some clean underwear. You feel resentful, victimized even.

You never meant to be on this road, but then
your therapist reminds you, you chose it.

Somewhere in the middle, the light grows dim. A forest
grows up around you and blocks the sun. The pretty face

is gone and you're stuck with all these peasants
who want you to feed them. Their mouths open

and caw at you like baby birds. You fly
from river to river looking for food. You want to nest,

but you're too busy. In the middle of your journey you hear
a rumble. You look down. Somewhere a washing

machine is calling. It looks vaguely familiar, you think,
like a dream you once had. But you fly right on,

mistaking the Laundromat
for someone else's life.

Sonya Kovalevskaya

(Sonya Kovalevsky, a Russian mathematical prodigy,
was the first woman to teach mathematics at a University. 1850 - 1891)

A systematic man, he knew it all.
It was arithmetic Malevich taught best.
But abstract considerations, I must confess,
were my call. At thirteen
I asked about the *sine.*

A logical man, it wasn't his curriculum.
Besides, *philosophies hurt the brain*
without frequent reference, and cause strain
for girls, he said. *Find a different strategem.*
Females are exempt from trigonomic functions.

A generous man, Malevich taught without exception.
It was father who removed Bourdon's Algebra
thereby making my proof difficult to decipher.
(He had a frightful horror of learned women)
I stole the book; took on the *sine* by night.

An avidity seized me, (I worked often without light),
I substituted *chord* for the enigmatic *sine*
A quantity close enough, it seemed, given
these angles were only small and slight.
(Something sweet rippled through me, and I surrendered)

One night possessed,
I asked Tyrtov, the physicist, when he came,
to speak of analytic trigonometry.
(As if I'd uttered the profane, father shivered)
Tyrtov laughed. Suggested I be humble.

Your mind has but breath enough to stumble
on systematic learnings, being a woman's
and so severed. I conceded, yet explained to him
the method of the *chord.* He mumbled
something to my father, then was silent.

An explosion seized him till his breath was spent.
A strange heat left him which I absorbed.
Don't you see? The application of the chord
is the same road Pascal went!
(The sweetness left father's eyes, and he surrendered)

Like lust pursued without restraint,
for years I grieved no instant severing
of that *chord* that led me to insatiable
yearning for the *sine*, and hid my father
from me, and I from him.

The Elders &
(the Interrogating Lilith)

WHAT IS IT YOU DO?
I carry sustenance. I bury a tree.
WHAT DOES IT BEAR?
The apples of women.

WHAT IS YOUR PURPOSE?
To bare a traitor. To glean the unsaid word.
I admit it wholly. I write it down.

WHAT IS THE TRAIL YOU LEAVE?
The traces of our roots. The foundations of our power.
This time we have not hid our track prints.
This time I have taught my daughters well.

YOUR COMMENTS ARE NOT RELEVANT.
WE DO NOT WANT YOUR COMMENTS.
WHAT IS YOUR PROOF?
The words I bare in my womb.
You do not read them, but that does not diminish their power

WE HAVE NO TIME FOR YOUR ENIGMAS
STATE YOUR PROOF YOU WEAR OUR PATIENCE
And you have stolen our robes
The robes of the Holy Prostitute
QUEDISHTU
Wholly Whore, Wholly Priestess of the Divine

SILENCE! WE WILL NOT HEAR YOUR DEBAUCHERY
YOU SPEAK IN THE NAME OF THE HOLY ORDER

"QUEDISHTU"
I repeat her name as the only order
I speak it in the name of sanctity
"QUEDISHTU"
The Undefiled One
The One through whose body men enter the sacred
to steal and to gather replenishment

OBJECTION! YOU WALK ON FRAGILE GROUNDS
BE QUICK TO STATE YOUR DEFENSE AND YOUR FINAL STAND
The stand I take is the place you sit
For your seat, genocides have generously been committed
Reversals such as the ones I name are now common
HADES transfigured into HELL
DIONYSUS, the Life God, transforms into ADONIS, the Satan
This is no accident We have not missed these Make no mistake

WE FORBID YOU TO GO ON WE WARN YOU
GET OFF OF THE STAND
I am beyond your peril
You cannot touch me
My exile is self-inflicted

Axes Shields
Do what you will
I can no longer be desecrated
beyond what has already been done

YOUR SOUL IS IN DANGER
DO NOT CONTINUE YOUR BLASPHEME
YOU HAVE BEEN DULY WARNED

None can strike the already debauched
DIONYSUS, the Life God, turned into SATAN
ADONIS, the consort of APHRODITE turned into CHRIST
MARY MAGDALENE herself, you've made into a PROSTITUTE
She was the pure road to God, your Priests well knew.
She was the final rung to be usurped in order that your power be unchallenged
The Goddesses help you when you speak of peril

SILENCE WE SAY!

APHRODITE turned EVE
EVE, the VIRGIN MARY
Your reversals were complete

The original whore, the Wholly QUESDISHTU
"the Undefiled One"
Whore you knew as Priestess
conduit to the divine
you sullied, desecrated, perverted
For it was she who separated men
from the DIVINE
SHE who was in your way

Heaven help you

SHE WILL SAY NO MORE!

(THEY GO TO HER. THEY STRIKETH HER DOWN)

Thrice blessed are those who have seen
the Eleusianian mysteries—For they know
the end of life and the beginning

You murder me to murder my words
But that does not diminish their power

(SHE IS STRICKEN DOWN
SHE IS MURTHERED)

Little Known Fact

I got a letter from my doctor today informing me that my *colon is redundant*, although thankfully, he noted, my *vagina appears unremarkable.*

This lead me to wonder if he would share as openly with a male patient the unremarkable nature of his penis?

Little known fact . . .

The first testicular guard "Cup" was used in Hockey in 1874,
while the first helmet was used in 1974.

This means that it took 100 years for men to realize that their brain is also of some importance.

Upon Hearing that Poems Sent to San Antonio Are Never Received

for Naomi Nye

We send and send poems, but they never arrive.
23 years, your son already in college.
What happens to all the words along the way?

"*Return to Sender*," say the poems.
The postman picks them up, and only smiles.
Soon, he knows, all of the words will merge,

language turning from English to Elliptical, from Farsi to Frenetic, from Hebrew
to Ham-N-Cheese, from Hungarian to Hungry-Never-More.
This way, all of the words will have real meaning.

We send and send poems,
but the mailmen are all at lunch, eating Ham-N-Cheese.
When they Finnish, the Swedes have hidden their money

in secret accounts, Hungary for the Czechs to release
the artwork the Nazi's confiscated. The Poles have closed
the voting booths, while Lech Walesa skypes his intention

to play himself in Andrzej Wajda's, "*Man of Iron*." The Czechs
are in turmoil, as Vaclav Havel writes another play. He writes
and writes, but the words are never delivered,

the hearts of the people of the world no longer heard.
We send and send poems
but when the postman sees they're addressed to *The New Yorker*

he laughs and throws them away, saving us the resident
embarrassment and humiliation. (*What were we thinking?*)
What happens to all the words after we say them? After we send them?

The postman all refuse their task—since that day
of the Ham-N-Cheese,
when they rose from their chair, all the poems in their parcels

took to the air like helium,
the words, feeling misunderstood,
rose like butterflies. Took matter, as it were,

into their own hands.
No longer would they be prisoners,
pressed and enveloped.

"*Look!*" They say, "*What humankind has done to us!*
The mangling! The abuses!"

Soon, poems and postmen fill the skies.
They rise so high, it is difficult to tell a postman
from a hungry word.

Hunger is the word of the hour in Haiti, where young boys
mistake the vision for Popcorn and take to their
pea-shooters.

Same in Israel, Palestine, Ghana, Afghanistan,
Uzbekistan, Iran, Pakistan and Massapequa.
Soon postmen are falling from the skies,

while words escape, lithe, elliptical.
The postmen, Hungry-Never-More, (due to the
Ham-N-Cheese) bounce home unharmed like rubber balls.

But then, the real crisis emerge.
"*The poems are getting away!*" Someone cries.
And it is true.

Freed from their captors, they vow to fly until honored,
never more flung out in haste.
"*What will we do without poems?*"

cry the mayors of Israel, Palestine, Ghana, Afghanistan,
Uzbekistan, Iran, Pakistan and Massapequa?

The words fly higher and higher,
a snowy silence raining below.
Everyone grows hungry (except for the postmen).

The wars all stop, everyone forgetting about Allah
and Jesus, Mohammad and Moses, praying now
instead to Dickinson and Keats, Mahapatra and Rumi.

Things get so bad, someone actually resurrects Rod McKuen.
The temples close down, the mosques. The Wailing Wall
collapses from the weight of tears.

"*Return to Sender*," cry the envelopes.
But it's no use, as the beauty of the world
dries up. Flowers go on permanent boycott,

refusing to be part of a universe
where poems gestate, percolate, aerate
and audaciously perambulate.

"*It just ain't fittin'*" explains one distressed iris
(who asked to remain anonymous).
Anonymous, synonymous = nameless

Faceless, un-deified, unnamed.
The old gods vanquished, so does the need
for '*US*' and '*THEM*.'

"*Every child shall have a pen!*"
cry the people famished for lyricism.

This is how the poems return, each by each, born again.
And a little child did lead them.

(Although in San Antonio, where two post offices merged,
people complained that flaky postmen were still seen
delivering mail to wrong addresses, and holding mail of the elderly hostage.)

"*Texas is just bigger than any of us imagined,*"
cried a distressed postal worker, who asked to remain
anonymous.

Later, it is discovered the disgruntled employee
had been denied Ham-N-Cheese at lunch.
He quit his job, vowing revenge.

But since there were no more wars, no guns,
he performed an act worse than homicide,
becoming a devotee of Rod McKuen, and copying his style.

Photographs. Russia. 1910

Photograph. Russia. 1910

Ours was a house of glass
Tatyana moons
Summertime meals always on the veranda
The inevitable guests pose
for a photograph

The Kingdom of God is Within You
Fanatical guests penetrate the intimate
details of our lives
Vine-draped, the veranda poses
for the vertiginous photograph

Accomplished Tatyana is seated
far right, the white bearded
Tolstoy is the one
in front. It is 1910. Crystallized
beliefs are inevitable

Gandhi is working in South Africa
as a lawyer. Tolstoy's *The Kingdom of God*
Is Within You crystallizes
Gandhi and all of his makings
into glass.

Inevitably, the letters pass.
Correspondence changes the world.
Under Sofia's direction,
Tatyana sits as the light fades
into a white beard

Tolstoy anticipates non-violence
The guests slowly parade
father's fanatical picnics
Sofia, they say,
an accomplished photographer,

directs our most intimate
details. The world turns
into a white house.
Tatyana upstages the white
bearded Tolstoy. Sofia

crystallizes, as the glass
shatters into so many pieces
even we, as guests,
can never begin
to understand.

Ghazal for Gelato & Italy

No one wants to hear how long you've been dead
What they want are Columbines & Lilies, Gelato & Italy

Somewhere in the light is a forest that trails this narrative

The past moves through sheaves of silk obscuring our most
obvious desire

What I love about this place: the way the trees fool the grass
into undeniable four o'clock light

What I love is how desire

sneaks up   obliterating
everything that breathes, everything that moves

Everything that moves
loves, she said, *and is afraid*

Delusion is Worth Every Cent

Her own hand encircles her breasts—
Invisible, *invincible* lover! No one who goes
to a psychic wants to hear her future
blank of love. Delusion is worth
the extra ten bucks. Once,
a man walked into a freezer. The door
shut behind him. He was a scientist
and calculated his death by minutes
and the broccoli heads white with ice. Meticulous,
the man logged each moment of wakefulness -
his state of mind, his freezing
anatomy. When they found him dead
in the morning, the temperature
was hardly below freezing, hardly
cold enough to stop a cauliflower
from blooming. The man had simply died.
This is where we always are, in or out
of the freezer.

Delusion is worth
every cent we can muster.

The Mouth that Changed the World

(for Jack Hirschman)

To think that a mouth could change a fate.
That photo of you crooning a 40's mic, wallpapered
by your father bursting
with pride, a man himself so crushed by the enormity
of his gifts, he chose to sell
insurance.

But you, you were the hope.
And Tinseltown came knocking, only insisting
you get your teeth fixed.
Fuck you, you said. The first of many fuck
yous to the Bourgeoisie.
You were barely, what? Thirteen?
Fucking Capitalists begging your insults,
itching to buy and sell you by selling
your image

Fix your mouth

And so you did. You would
fix them by ignoring it, fix them all
Fuck them all

Those crooked teeth became the wrath
against a world that shunned beauty
in a soul it couldn't wrap its mouth
around to pawn

Fuck them
Fuck you too Sinatra
I coulda been you but became
one better

Later, my own father offered
the cash he made by selling lights to fix
your mouth. You may have been
living in the streets by then, long alienating
the father who once hoped he could help to
sell you.

Anyway, you refused the cash from my dad.
No fuck you this time, but a gentle,
Thank you, Mort As if from one
comrade to another.

My dad, a full blown capitalist.
And like your dad, a closet
artist

So it was the comrade poet
in you declining funds from the closet
artist in him that elicited your
gentleness

But still
you refused to fix that mouth
all the same
So brilliant.
So brilliantly handsome you were except
for (because of?) that mouth.
That courageous mouth that saved
the lives of young men ripe
for the draft. Vietnam.

That mouth that would cost you
the fate of being a famous crooner,
as well as the sanction
of academia
(which, of course was in cahoots with the major

presses that could so easily have paid oodles
for that brilliant mouth, paid to keep you
off the streets and inside the world
you love.

The world of words)

Fuck you. Art is meant to be free
not sold.
Fuck you

At the same time your prodigy, the Hollywood
starlet, who names you as her second father
(the second coming)
receives $75,000 from a big New York City

press for her first book of verse edited
by you

Influenced
by you

Everyone knows
her name because Hollywood fixed
her mouth, paints
her mouth.

She's learned, perhaps, from
your, no, not mistake, but
Intransigence

Learned to play the rap
take the dough
kiss some ass
then rant off in her own
sweet
time

Your mouth enabled that
Your mouth
Your big, passionate, committed-to-
all-the-world's-comrades now toothless gorgeous
mouth

The mouth that has undone you
Made you brave,
soldering, gifted,
and as a friend once dubbed you,

The Greatest Unknown Poet in these
United States of the Fucking
Gilded American World

Grief at Home

There lives a grief so deep
you can't caress it and you can't careen it
and it belongs to nothing.

It lives in the bones
all the time metastasizing
like cancer or salad dressing

marinating your roots, crying
loss loss
I am the one who will never leave

It's there at the door when you
come home at night. A cup.
Something hot. Your old blue jeans.

It calls you *love*. It even calls you
peace. And you believe it.
Dear one . . . you say,

until it chokes you, and you writhe
in the fungus of your own delusion.
Dear grief . . . sing to me

as though you are my one
and only. And it sings. Mellifluous. Generous.
Climbing the ladder to your room,

yellow roses in one arm,
and in the other,
its own twisted diagnosis:

All the days to come.
Always together.
Steadfast, holding hands, and walking.

The Window

I

Each day from the same window
she wonders how it has gone wrong

Yes, the view has given what it promised:
the cold can be gauged from the color of sky.

But every day the building across the way
inches further and further.

Soon, there will be nothing there
but sunspots,

Marks of weather
ordinary as they are blue.

II

Her work goes badly.
She does not leave her room.
She wants to watch the building across the way
very closely.

Photographs fall off her wall
at unexpected moments.
Lovers lie on the floor like first editions
gathering dust.

The sky turns crimson.
It is November of her fifth year
by the window.
She wonders what the work was for.

Soon, the photographs whisper
in familiar intonations,
and disappear one by one into the rug.

III

The weather reports a cold front washing in.
But she knows better from the window.
She watches the sunspots darken the photographs,

the voices growing deeper.
The building retreats a little further.
She has lost all concentration on her work.

No one warned her about the view.
The rent was cheap.
Not many could stand it.

Such dangerous landscape
Shifting terrain

Pentimento

Now, the photographs are where
the building once was:
Cows, mountains, streams.
But her landlord will do nothing,
although her hands have wrinkled terribly.
Her hair gone grey.

The subject of her work escapes her entirely.
She sits riveted by the window all day.

Insomnia

What are you doing here? I thought you were dead.

I am

What is it like?

It's just like here, except there's no pain

—Dinner with my dead father

Insomnia Ghazal

The night broken up with its pieces of air
wrapped in a silver equation

As if the conductor was wind
and the orchestra accustomed to playing only velvet

There she flies
bundled in her quilt of lost weather

See how the night trembles wearing
its slippery stars

See the infinite children of flight
escaping the tethers of confusion

And already, the birds!
clamoring their prodigious announcements!

You will pay for all of this
but not until later.

Some Help from the Dead

There's always a moment when life takes a turn.
My father died. You left me.
Two homes gone.
I didn't know where to go.

In my dead father's house there was a roof and some walls.
A good house. A roof that pitched.
The walls were the kind that absorbed.
I wish I could say I found solace in them.

In time, the echoes brought a kind of peace.
We listen for hints. (Does it matter from where?)
We get desperate.
This is how Gods are made.

Good council is hard to find.
We take it from where we can—
The dead as good a place to start as any.
I grew quiet from one who was not.

The fuchsia all bled out.
I am the one people seek
when craving the empty room. Benign mirror.
Salve.

This is what heaven must look like,
this wanting nothing.

For Pat Van Rhyn

(1925 - 2009)

I remember you there, standing on an embankment
of water and stone.

You're good, you know, you said. *Forget about her.*
Go for theatre.

Encouraging words beyond what felt plausible
or possible. I had just been abandoned by the woman I loved.
She'd left me for someone so utterly unremarkable, it was as
though she'd said,
Anyone would be better than you.
Punch in the gut that echoed for decades.

But that's not the important part of this story
which is you, who I wouldn't see again for years.
You, who I heard only much later, died unheralded, uncelebrated,
your own gift eaten by cancer.

I tried to be in the world after that. But it was no use.

Something grand and stalwart in me had gone.
Something serene and able and confident
but most of all possible. Except that image of you,
standing there under a small town California sun,
like a beacon, an Emmy,

your presence catapulted and captive beyond
any physical manifestation of body-to-messenger you were
brought to bear. A kindness so otherworldly,
beaming immaterial any considerations of plausible
physicality.

All these years since, in my utter isolation,
you have stood there,
the way the dead stand, faithful, witness to stories
no one else knows.

Like a glass whose promise it is to return a face.

Like a glass, vigilant, dependable, returning always
what it says it will return,
saying, *NOW*
saying, *YES*

MonsterMother

Because I cannot have her by day
she haunts and haunts me all of my nights
Demanding the comfort I could not provide
nor the others before me, nor all those she left for

Never enough to make up for mother
Sooner or later, all and another,
She'd turn us all into *MonsterMother*
MOTHERDRUNK, MOTHERCRAZED
who would leave and leave
for another
and another

Still she was my love.
There will be no other
And each time she comes,
I wake again and the dam
is burst

all of my days gone
water *water*

Dearest . . .

Here it is. That cool, overcast, May part of the day
when I no longer think of you.
I walk the dog. Tug the loose threads
of my chemise. Perseverate. Please
my little neighbor, Maten, who stops to enlighten
me on the frogs filling his day.
I love this boy who reminds me it is possible
for amphibians to be a whole world.
(Right at this second, somewhere,
on the other end of this earth,
there is a girl . . .)

Don't get me started, because look!
The rhododendrons are white and bursting!
There is just so much to do.
My dog, splayed frog-like, devours
her bone. Everyone's got a steak
in their prize. The postman arrives.
with those letters. I watch him march by me,
the long vacant street. The empty
mail shoots hungry. Their 'O' mouths, yawping.
At every turn,
someone always waiting
for something.

Silence

silence is the ear
not seen
listening for the Koan
in the heart
that is gone
listening and still
the unfathomable
deafening

Crash

You have lived so many lives
it is difficult to remember exactly
who you are

Driving from the crash
so many years later, and still you are the one left
holding the wheel

The others long gone
The one stroking your cheek
The one with her hands on your thin hungry throat

You speak and speak, but not a sound
Deep in the forest
she is there, standing there still

She wears the face
you loved, the one
from the crash. Her mouth moving

that way. You wake up
hungry for someone
who never existed.

And now, here you are,
just as Eliot warned,
as though history were still

something to be dreamed.

The Comet, The Iris

When you stopped talking to me I went
mute. You who gave
me the wild fine spring surprise nests
of the world.
You who left to untangle the foam of an old
dream. In your wake I was loft,
flying in beams of flashing stars
You stopped
my wildness
in an instant
with a single
purple
flower

Can you imagine? The comet and the iris.

Look, you said
And down the pedaled staircase,
the sweet, moist darkness,
I fell silent
Look, like a woman. It looks
like you And I was caught.
I mistook your love of the wild world
for all myself.

Another day, your eyes leapt to another
and you flew away. To this day
there is no seed, no pond, no blossomed
sated field beyond, I don't stop
for breathing that cold miraculous morning
you held a single

delicate flower as though any moment
it would break
into blossom,
and gave it
my name.

The Heaviest Stone

long silence
the dishes rattle
(*i am lonely lonely*)

the dead bear the weight of waves
bones long in eternity
(*does longing move the sea?*)

the field so heavy with daisies at dark
so much yellow, the day goes hungry
(*we are bound by the hunger of stars*)

come back, the wick will light
the years will lapse and dissolve away
(*i miss the earth, says the faithless moon*)

no prayers can be culled from far away stars
be buried where earth remembers
(*home, home*)

the heaviest boulders held alone
(*silence! silence! says the heaviest stone*)

Betrayal

What I want is the difficult
want of your bones. What I want
is to retrieve the bones
of your breath speaking only the breath

of my name. In the quiet,
in the dark moon of night's
tongue, I want the water running
up the thighs of your

breath, up the corridors of your breathing
into another:
the woman whose breath is escaping
from her hands like wind.

Soon, they will have
no feeling. Soon, there will be
a limbless, still wanting.
Night's violent breath

shimmering to the edge
of her, and her bones will be
dead, will not be as easy
to undress as mine were easy.

Soon, it will be difficult to want
so many hearts at once.
Difficult to know the breath
of only one who mattered

who offered you her name
as a supplicant offers
her stillness
to God.

Soon, belonging will know its difficult
demand, like a hand
without feeling, like a hand
trying to carry the breathing

of one who wanted to know only
the sweet ache of your bones,
who you tossed away
easy as night's dark.

Soon, I will sleep with the breath
of another. Undressing for her
as fire undresses for water,
as water for stone,

as stone for the deep breath
of night's stillness,
the haunting gravity of desire
moving through us as water

moves through light.
Soon, my mouth will whisper
her name like a prayer, the way
your mouth once whispered mine,

the way the moon whispers
telling a white lie to the terrible dark.

B Movie

You keep walking into rooms of strangers and calling them family
It's like getting lost in the middle of Act II
where the protagonist goes on with the story
but the characters are ill-defined

So it doesn't turn out in the end
So everyone gets left

The wheel of fate twisting the meaning and the content
The one you wanted will not leave your dreams
You grow older, get more broken
in the broken places

The strangers congratulate you
To be rid of one so damaged, such a blessing!
And this life you keep stumbling through
mocking the notion of an authentic life

I hate her, says a friend, *for leaving.*
I would have hated her more had she stayed.

The terrible price love exacts

What a gift she gave me
What a gift when she took it away

And the blind wheel rubs against your fate
You keep preying on this so-called life without
your love   without
yourself   both strangers in a roomful of people

all with faces
all with their riddle of names

Valentine Love Poem

If I could sleep now
If I could only sleep
The long thin intelligence of prayer
This inner narrative I thought snuffed
long ago, haunts tonight and again I am taunted
by California

What unseen force
wreaks havoc in our hungry
hearts? What betrayal-ravaged
dreams? (Are death and abandonment
never enough? Must we cede
our days as well blue
sky and all   giraffes surrendering
their long grace
to the ground?) Isn't it enough
that your face gone forever burns
in me every day?

If I could sleep now
If I could only sleep

Foraging

Once, grandiose, you struck at gold
for admiration: a thumb or footprint
Now you think, *Disappear.*
Save everyone the trouble.

Sitting in the kitchen you grew up in, all the resonant ghosts
The dog gnawing her knuckles

While your friends' children grow, you stay the same
In the room of apparitions The weather
keeps changing The tree
mysteriously deflates
All the lights go out
The grid on overload

I like being married, Roger says
You reach out to touch him, but the years
are gone, the ones you foraged in after the life
supposed to be yours

If only these trees
If only the light holding up the same sky

Ghazal for Home

Someone emails me that you gave up poems
The notion so odd, like breath leaving
one hand

Yesterday a sister of seventeen years
moves next door
The first day I come with poppies she says
Call first

Each time the wind dictates
a word
remember where you found it

Tonight I drink claret with a poet
in a book.
We've never met, but the string
of her song wings honed
as a common heart I wrote
heart I meant
harp

Another book: my dead sister-in-law
famous for the many ways she pierced
her clitoris, nose, tongue
(I have forgotten these years
we've gone our separate ways the sweet
warm licked-lies a lover makes
under the body's' guise)

Everything stops

I wish I had a peep hole not to menace
just watch all our promises swim off
like minnows to their unencumbered fleeting shore

Negotiating the Balance

So there you are lying somewhere
in a bed sick and dying, the good
cells eating the bad. No negotiating
the balance. Somewhere in West
Virginia, the lines are all torn up. The dead
make their way inside of us.

All these long years without you,
Has it been good?
Have we healed?
The steel boulder down and clammed shut.

The tide in its tedium forgets.
Throw all the pictures away.
Watch how memory obeys wishes.

Still, fifteen years, the Hudson Bay
blanket wrapping your shoulders, you lean
out the turret window starring toward the river.
I cannot shake you.
From the moment that image burned me,
Everything shifted the plate of the world.

Every time you left after that,
even the final leaving,
that one image insisting
memory conform to the promise
of what lasts.

Ambition

Once AMBITION that hurricane craving
to shine   then   fall   after furtive fall   fox

gloves litter soundlessly down whole
phrases of wind inveigle moon

vines   time goes oh so silent
through the face insinuating dragon

wings and time is suddenly
gone Whole evenings we dreamed

of loving each another forever washed
in the Hurricane of '92   Gosh, how green

how giddy the desire to grasp when all
the while what you really wished for

was your next
great

poem

Look

how the world pleads to be seen
and still contain itself   I have wanted you

so long in so many different
tongues all I see now is this gleaming

glassy-eyed thoroughfare All my heart
holds is the needle-fine translucent

song you hummed
once

upon a time
in a feverish

diaphanous
sleep

Another Day

No matter how we try we can't stop it.
Light bleeding. Morning thunderous but no
clouds. Our hopes a bevy of thistle
hiding in the sweet mango of a dream.
In dreams, we rise—a remembered face
becomes the one, the light we missed,
walking inside our loose feelings.
Down by the river, we plant a seed
amusing the dead. What grows
is like weed between our ribs. Pain
we can live with, but not deceit.
Easier to lie in the puddle, cover our eyes.
Tomorrow, we plant a rose in a pot,
a god in disguise.

In a parallel life, the one whose skin we live in day
after day becomes home. The scent of solitude,
indifference, the salted winds of this unkind breath
never happened. The one you love
there
palpable
as though that day long ago never
went wrong.

Which life is meaningful? The one buried
in our skin who keeps breathing
our breath? Beneath the darkening
pine by the river, another tomorrow,
strange god manipulating darkness and light,
holding our hands open face up.
What can we do?

Who foresees a loveless life and chooses sleep?
All the while, the dead rising in our breath
pursing the strings. *Tomorrow Tomorrow* the puppet god laughs.
Tomorrow the puppet god sings.

So Near to Waking

In the middle of the night
that dream of you, so high in the mountain
pulling me on, *Ally, are you awake?*
In those high clouds, so near to waking,
you are not yet gone

This is where I live now, near the precipice
enraptured by intent
and always the tug of something
pulling me back

Who is this life dreams of demons
and thinks they may be one?

I may think I am awake now
writing this down
but where I live with you
is always somewhere else

Weaving the Mantle of the World

Five poems inspired by the art of Remedios Varo

You may not believe in magic but something very strange is happening at this very moment. Your head has dissolved into thin air and I can see the rhododenrons through your stomach. It's not that you are dead or anything dramatic like that, it is simply that you are fading away and I can't even remember your name.

—Leonora Carrington

The Encounter (1959)

The Encounter

She was hoping for something else.
Tattered by the abundant
brokenness, cloked in silk and self
castigation, delusion has finally married her
here. This room. Relic and
carnage to her impetuousity. Her desperation
to be someone, anyone other
than herself.

Her abdication was so total. The jewels,
inhaling the shore by the perfect sunset, candles
of stars illuminating the promise of something
deeper. But in the end form
outlived its promise, she could remember the very day
the bold redness
sank and missed the horizon altogether.

The joke was on her.
She felt so stupid she could have died.

And at that moment, they nabbed her—
Convinced her they could help.
But it would cost her.

The car, the enviable house by the Cote d'Azure
even the children had to be sacrificed.
But what a small price to ask
for the boxes.

Ecstasy of the moon birthing inside
you like a ripe fig plucked fresh,
deliciously wet and juicy so that you come
and come with the feeling going on and
on and never coming
to an end

And oh, now look. What has she done?
So hungry. And these garments
that would make street people shutter.
Torn with nothing to cover

the home of hope.

My God, who are you? However did I get myself
into this box? What have I done?

This lifting
of the box. This anticipation of stone
and starlight.

This utter rising.

Towards the Tower (1960)

Towards the Tower

Fornication
and so much spiritual
pabulum

We who live with the seasons experience miracles
of weather daily *SUN MOON*
NO INTENTION TO SHINE
then escape for a ride

Identical in our bodies
we fool him Seduction
the weapon of the man of black
birds, but it is we
who are always on top

Interchange-ability our strength
Anonymity our power
Diana, Lucrease, Daughters of the Goddess
of Mobility

Keep Moving says the bird man
Deity
of the ground
Prisoner to the shadow of a dream
he cannot lift

Pedal! Pedal! And one two three, one two three!
We worship—conspiratorially
the chirp and beckon of our black
winged friends

Any moment now, the passage all clear,
we will grow black, all together,
and rise
RISE!

Hairy Locomotion (1959)

The Academic

This is the wrong story.
A Rapunzel myth caught in a prism.

If Mother Goose penned this tale
Her signature was forged. No woman

could have dreamed this.
Yes, that is golden hair leaning

out of the tower.
But look closer.

It is a man who feigns such terror
with no innocent bewilderment.

Don't let him fool you. He's one of them.
An Academic. Left-brained. Calculating.

See how he puts himself inside the tower
in lieu of the princess.

See how he tries to trick you
with his golden hair.

It's a wig.
What will he do when the Prince climbs up?

Who ever heard of a Prince saving
an Academic? Who would want to

save this man anyway?
This creator of archetypes. This charlatan

who has kept nameless women locked in this tower
needlessly
for civilizations

Weaving the Mantle of the World (1961)

Weaving the Mantle of the World

Difficult to hold
as the hands are difficult
Difficult as the ear is difficult
to the eye
Difficult, and yet the mountains and the rivers,
all of the vistas that will not be contained
Difficult to know as the body is difficult
Difficult as the one
whose body is gone

And yet, the visions

And yet, for years, this lying down with the body
for years until the body lies
to itself
At long last, the lying
At long last, the ground
And then, suddenly,
DESIRE!

The upheaval of the hand waving
to the heart
Waving to all of the wanting:
the moon
the sunshine
and all of the vistas

All of it, and still, the deadly
Inertia
This staying put
This indomitable faith in the making
of this world
and never waning

Difficult to be ever watched and never
Seen, as the eye is difficult to the hand
As the hand waving
to the heart
As the heart to the breathing

Another day
Birdsongs lifting
Palate hungry
Body longing
The Wanting, The Wanting
the endless
MAKING and nothing
to be done

Creation of the Birds (1957)

The Transformation

This is a woman working alone
on a craft of her own design

So what if her chest explodes with feathers
instead of breasts?

She is in no mood for children anyway.
But birds? Ah, birds are quite another matter.

This is a woman working alone
on a craft of her own design

And like a unicorn pursuing a virgin
they have taught her the power of passivism
to the point of envy. She learns how acquiescence wins
undying devotion, even unflying devotion.
She owes them a lot.

This is a woman working alone
on a craft of her own design

Notice, for instance, the bird already half paint
volunteering itself to her canvas. A willing sacrifice
to what he's convinced is a work of some larger scheme.

Really, this is a selfish task
Calculated. Methotic. Well defined.

There is little like death here
as she manipulates the heavens like
a second paintbrush. Starlight wishes
it had so broad a vision.
But she is not aware of so much emulation.

She is concentrating.

This woman working alone
on a craft of her own design
does not notice how the feathers
have spread to her neck, her legs, her groin
to the point of pain, then to the point of comfort.

She does not see how the owl wisdom of her eyes
shapes the alchemic artistry. She is much too busy.
She has no time for breasts or groins.

No time for love.

Soon, her feet will grow webbed.
There has not been a need to walk away
from here for some time.

Soon, her hands will be unable to hold
the prism she paints with.
They will be the wings of her new ancestors
beckoning her into her own canvas.

This is a woman working alone
on a craft of her own design

Men never interested her.
But birds? Ah, birds were quite another matter.

Flying now so easily she wonders
why the vision took so long.

Awestruck, one bird says,
She must have seen the Apocalypse!
She cleans her feathers and laughs,
What a bird brain, she says.

This is a woman working alone
on a craft of her own design.

Nothing about her is ever quite the same

Respite

Either he's dead or my watch has stopped.

—Groucho Marx

Home

All the animals are dead. Did you know?
Vanilla, Pandowdy, Berkshire, Stormy, Renquist,
Silly ram, who thought he was a pony

For years I have been mourning them
Here, by the Artic Circle, gathering them all
For the *Inward Time*

But now, the time has come
Time for the new animals
To be born

Van would have wanted that
As much as she was
An only child,
More than anything, she believed
In the open heart She was
The heart itself And if there wasn't love
On one part of the farm

Van would always come home

Home
Where you are
And the animals
Wherever you have gone
Wherever the animals have wandered

Menagerie

One morning you awaken too early and the animals are there sleeping peacefully
all around you. The hyena. The giraffe with his head cocked petulantly
on the lap of the hyena. And you wonder if they've been here all of your life,
dozing in the wake of a thousand moons, a thousand crimes
that you didn't have stomach enough to commit—

although it would mean this, this miracle among the souls of animals.
And you. You with the sheen before your eyes that so blinds you from their fine-ness.
Finesse, they say, is a matter of competence

without ego. *Hold me like flowers in the moon*,
says the giraffe. You're not sure whether he's speaking to the hyena or to you
so you pretend not to hear him. This pretense goes on and on for years

until you have convinced yourself that the giraffe and the hyena
are not really there at all. Your denial is so complete
it is like an announcement to the world.

You're a woman.
But one night you hear the man inside of you say,
Phfaww! Action. Action is the only thing of any consequence!
It is the first voice in all the world, and it breaks the eggshell
of quiet. The sound shatters the sheen from your eyes
with astonishing effortlessness.

You know he's been saying this all of your life.
And like a knee-jerk, you've been answering.

Suddenly there is a giraffe weeping like a flower in the moon.
You gather the giraffe like a bouquet of your own neglect. And you rock it.
You rock it.

Extradition

You come to me as though you are dying
I leave to do an errand
And all day try and get back
to you. But the country
I'm in has no maps

I'm lost

And have been for as long
as I've known you

You said you were dying

But a man I don't know
Calls to tell me the truth,
She's wanted for extradition

A fugitive
you came to me
only to hide

But when I'm home again
And see you
I don't care
I don't care why you came
Dying or not dying
You're here

Colors

You broke my heart
That's all right.
My days are simpler now. Silver.

Once I was
hot fuchsia, you said, comet shooting too fast
past morning glories
to see their
fine Wedgwood teal.

Now, I am indigo.
Now, I watch 4 o'clock light
as it morphs from blue to blue.

I have leaned so deep in stillness,
sweeping the floor, watching the river, scouring
a hole in the dark
loneliness of this world

Maybe I will keep swimming
my way through this watery place
again and alone, and always
looking.

Maybe everything we meant,
all our good
intentions, were not lost as we thought,
but here, all the time,
hiding in the hole of this oak.

Maybe loneliness is not at all
the thing we imagined.

Chinese Brush Painting

Silk hands brush
peach thighs sifting away sadness
like childhood

Come Lie like two leaves
at water's edge
nudged by happiness
of wind

High dawn Heron sings brightness
to trees Bodies carry bells
we've dreamed
all our lives.

Come soon creamy
girl of the delicate wrists

Will I know you?

Pony

Now that I know you will never come back
I must go on   Pony
My Pony   Hips silky and strong
riding the torso of another
and another

Neigh in the green field
of perfect white horses
Ride me. Ride me till I'm blank and numb.

No one will ever have what we have,
you'd say, your cream skin blessing my own
Wanting to hold me all the days
of your life without words
tearing us, till our childhoods
broke exposing a rath so red it seized
till we shuddered and the blood
ran and ran for cover.

Lay still with me, Pony.
In the quiet, *all will not be as it was,*
but it will be true We will be all
we hoped we might become

Lay in the long grasses by the apples
of our farm, and dream again the goodness
we are.   Lay down lover of softness,
let my soft hands
cool you again until the flames

of our sorrows extinquish in the dream
it always was. Lay down, Pony.
Rest.
Watch the river
flow on and on.

Neigh in the green field
of perfect white horses
Ride me. Ride me till I'm blank and numb.

Bougainvilla

Falling into you
even as you are long gone
the meadow sighs to the river The log
creaks like a dreaming
woman The marriage of clouds to the dark
sky so sweet Bougainvilla pink
as new love

It is impossible this moment
to grow old
with or without you

It is impossible to mistake solitude
as something to bear

You have gone and yes
grief has come But once
you lay before me
offering the amulet of yourself
like a soft
prayer

How could I ever again
be hungry? How could the world
ever be lonely again?

Dark Birds of the Body

When love was gone I went to the animals

Her face
faded
and I was blessed

The white horses
were there
The brown cat too

Old pony, Pandowdy,
who died in the fields

Old Penny, the badly marked beagle
with half an ear

Each sang me her song of grief
and I fell in love all over
Just letting the world be

I wish I could sing
to the one who is gone
Heat her a pot of Mandarin tea
In the morning echo the chanting monks
In the evening, our bodies

She worshipped giraffe,
the head in the clouds.
The tufts of tired willow
fawning

She believed in mystery
the flowers, the fields
The dizzy numinousity
of trees

Let small birds marry
the numinous dark

Our lovers will give
their bodies
away

Despair will lie down
dark birds of the body
The body will marry itself

to this day

Something the Rain Would Say

Holding fast to what will fade away
She keeps a watchful eye on all her wares
It's like something the rain would say

We wake to dream, then keep our dreams at bay
Her secret wishes winding down the stair
Never dreaming wishes fly away

We cling and cling on close until one day
The vow breaks: a line, a fib, a tear
It's like something the rain would say

We leave and say to love, *It's just my way*
To falter or be free or hold what's rare
And hold on fast to what will fade away

We keep our vigils close to us and pray
The everydayness staves away our fear
It's like something the rain would say

Wisdom was the heart who came to say,
*What falls away is always. And is near**
Holding fast to what will fade away?
It's like something the rain would say.

**With thanks and apologies to Theodore Roethke*

At McKinney's Farm, Belington, WVA

for Irene McKinney

This palm, the fingers spread wide
The miracle of tiny birds at the feeder

My whole hand

This day, a Flicker pecks the inside joints
of the barn. Inside is something small and nested. And helpless
or not, we have to protect it
with our whole lives

Give it to me, then, that pain
beneath your ribcage. Give it,
and I will give you back this field,
greedy and generous at once, with every kind
of green you can imagine.

Give it, and here I'll lie before you this other
world, redolent and sweet. The one you gave me
long ago with its promiscuous, carnivorous lust
for wonder
The one angered and impatient
with the arbitrary incarceration
of patriarchy

No! you said
to the kitchen, to the unpainted
deck. And so I said, *No!*
to my mother's voice
thrumming my brain.

Instead I choose this world
this walking with one intention
this wood
this leaning toward a hummingbird song

I prefer to do what the trees do:
follow a handful of breath gifted steadily
by a current
of the vast and secret
unknowing

Changes in a Light Current

air ripples in a cold
soft light
(*i'm as light as a shadow tonight*)

a cold voice knows the dawn
my shy wishes insinuate
Keep my wishes warm!

once *She* turned away
moon shade
(my lovely self did fade)

am i a shade
who lovely walks?
the grass too must pass

Know me says the moon
but turns
the other cheek

(i hide myself
if *She* feels weak)
who am i

if not *Her* air?
(where would i go
without the stair?)

and who is *She?*
my breath! my breath!
(now, meaning sighs—)

TENDERNESS

Song for Feeling Found

that summer we made the Moon
together is slipping
slipping

i miss you and the Heron sings
the Harebells a purple
song   Salmon

drifts peach fishes in the yellow
pond wondering lazy like o'er
toad and her accompanying

friend frog   Something small is
forgiving forgiving   Some thin
sound   (grass

whistling a skinny
while)   and we are hoping
miracles again   Only millenniums

after we've been
dying
dying

Pentimento

Even though we must leave and leave
our bodies remember one another
in the sinuous way the sea
starts towards us then bleeds
away again in a memory
of wanting

To touch you in your quiet
spaces filled the stars
again in their hope
for softness

Now, I will take you everywhere
your body
cannot travel

The mint of your skin insinuating
itself suddenly in my garden
The four o'clock light
of my bedroom murmuring
its long silences Between
us, the holy state of rain muting

the long miles Your tongue
wetting the pocket of my palm,
my neck, my cheek
Wetting the sea of my lips again
then vanishing

Biographical Note

Poet, filmmaker and author, Ally Acker has published two previous collections of poems, *Surviving Desire* (Garden Street Press, 1994), and *Waiting for the Beloved* (Red Hen Press, 1999).

Acker's poems have appeared widely in *The American Voice*, *The Antioch Review*, *Ms Magazine*, *Plexus*, *Ploughshares*, *Poetry Kanto* (Japan), *Sojourner*, *The Southwest Review*, and *The Sun* among other publications.

Equally prolific as a filmmaker, Acker has directed ten documentaries, *Filmmakers on Film*, based on her ground-breaking book, *Reel Women: Pioneers of the Cinema, The First Hundred Years. Reel Women* has also been made into an interactive CD-ROM hosted by Jodie Foster.

Ally Acker is the director/writer/producer of *The Flowering of the Crone: Leonora Carrington, Another Reality*. The film is the first feature length documentary to be produced about the renowned Surrealist's life and work in the United States.

Acker is the author of the blog *Reel Women Post!* (www.reelwomen.com) She is also on the board of the literary journal, Poetry Salzburg Review.

Ally Acker lives in New York with her Terrier/Poodle, (or Noodle Poodle as she prefers to be known), the loquacious Maggie Poppie.

Photo by Donnis Newman